THIS BOOK BELONGS TO

The Huntington for Kids

A Kaleidoscope of Books, Art, and Nature

KATHLEEN THORNE-THOMSEN

Huntington Library   San Marino, California

Huntington Library Press, Peggy Park Bernal, Director
1151 Oxford Road   San Marino, California 91108
626-405-2172   www.huntington.org

With special thanks to: Charley Allen; Armstrong Nursery; Matthew Barrett and Jim Walker, Los Angeles MTA Library; Bellefontaine Nursery; Andre Chaves; Cathy Cherbosque; Kitty Connolly; Doreen Hambleton; Bunny Pierce Huffman; Charles Kohlhase; Sean Lahmeyer; Judith Leavelle-King; John Marquette; Rafael Mejia-Lopez, Herzog Transit Services; Paul Meyers; Holly Moore; The Nethercutt Collection; Jim Paden; James and Graham Pulliam; Renee Shepherd, reneesgarden.com; Henry Sherrod; Dale Trader; Mark Vahrenwald; Ardis Willwerth, Pasadena Museum of History.

Photography Credits: Huntington Library Media Bank: pages 2, 12, 12 & 13 bottom, 20, 21, 24 left, 28, 29 top, 30, 31, 32, 33, 34, 35, 36, 37, 38, 39, 41 left & bottom, 42, 43, 44, 45, 46, 47, 48, 49, 56, 57, 59 top left, 62 top left, 63 bottom, 64, 65 top, 66, 67, 70 left. The Huntington Library has granted permission for the reproduction of images based on its collections. Author: pages 3, 4, 5, 6, 7, 8, 9, 10 & 11 center, 13 top, 14, 15, 16, 17, 18, 19, 22, 23, 24 right, 29 bottom, 30 & 31 center, 40, 41 top right, 44 & 45 center, 51, 52, 53, 55 top, 62 bottom, 64 & 65 center, 68, 69; Lisa Blackburn: title page, page 25; Andre Chaves: page 55 bottom; Bunny Pierce Huffman: illustration pages 26 & 27; Charles Kohlhase, pages 64 & 65 bottom; Pasadena Museum of History: pages 59, 60, 61, 63 top right, 70 right; courtesy of the California State Railroad Museum: page 71 top; Jim Walker, Los Angeles MTA Library: pages 71 lower left, 72 photo; Mark Vahrenwald: map, pages 72 & 73.

The author and the publisher disclaim all liability incurred in connection with the use of the information contained in this book.

Library of Congress Cataloging-in-Publication Data
Thorne-Thomsen, Kathleen.
The Huntington for kids : a kaleidoscope of books, art, and nature / Kathleen Thorne-Thomsen.
     p. cm.
     ISBN 978-0-87328-224-6 (alk. paper)
  1. Henry E. Huntington Library and Art Gallery—Juvenile literature.
  2. Huntington Botanical Gardens—Juvenile literature.
  3. Huntington, Henry Edwards, 1850–1927—Juvenile literature.
  4. Rare book libraries—California—San Marino—Juvenile literature.
  5. Art museums—California—San Marino—Juvenile literature.
  6. Botanical gardens—California—San Marino—Juvenile literature.
  I. Title.
     Z733.H5T45 2007   026'.0909794'93—dc22
     2007044418

This book is dedicated to Henry Edwards Huntington, a visionary business-man who created the first urban transportation system for Los Angeles. It is also dedicated to the future of an even stronger urban transportation system for our great city.

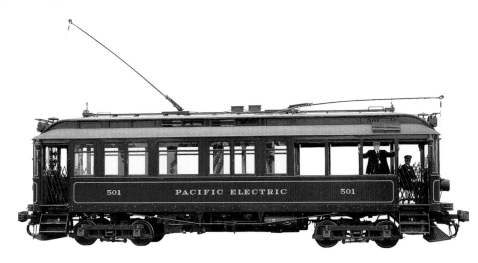

Introducing the Huntington

Henry Huntington's hard work and his generous philosophy of giving back to the community created the Huntington Library, Art Collections, and Botanical Gardens, a place for all to enjoy. *The Huntington for Kids* pictures only a small amount of the vast treasure chest of plants, trees, paintings, sculpture, decorative objects, books, manuscripts, and historical artifacts contained within the Huntington's collections. Turn the page to learn about the Botanical Gardens (page 2), the Huntingtons and the house they lived in (page 24), the Art Collections (page 30), the Library (page 42), and Henry Huntington's life and the role he played in the history of Southern California (page 56).

The Beginnings of Mr. Huntington's Gardens

In 1903 Henry Huntington bought the San Marino Ranch, which had impressed him on his first visit to Southern California in 1892. The ranch had belonged to the family of Benjamin Davis "Don Benito" Wilson, the first mayor of Los Angeles. It was an extraordinary place. The San Marino Ranch was more than three times as big as the Huntington is today and included most of what is now the city of San Marino. The northern area was covered with native plants, California oak trees, and brush-filled canyons. Springs and creeks flowed into natural lakes. The southern area was partly pasture and partly planted with fruit orchards.

The orchards produced commercial crops of oranges, lemons, apricots, figs, and olives. Henry needed someone to help him care for his large ranch, so he hired a very talented ranch superintendent. Together they experimented with new crops to find out which would thrive in the soil and climate, and bring the best price in the marketplace.

Jay Last Collection

2

One day Henry showed his ranch superintendent several "alligator pear" seeds (avocado pits) that were given to him by a chef at a Los Angeles restaurant. Henry had enjoyed tasting this fruit and wanted the superintendent to plant the "alligator pear" seeds. This experimental planting on the San Marino Ranch led to the development of one of the first commercial avocado groves in California.

Does the outside of this avocado remind you of alligator skin? Is the shape similar to the shape of a pear?

Suitable plants for the ranch were gathered from all over Southern California and Mexico. Sometimes Henry bought plants from nurseries as far away as New Jersey and London, England. Once a plant was located, it was immediately paid for, dug up, and moved back to the ranch. Henry bought an entire Japanese tea garden in Pasadena and moved it—buildings, plants, and trees—to his ranch.

Henry continued to develop the gardens by adding a rose garden, a cactus garden, a collection of prehistoric cycad plants, and, for his family's meals, a large fruit and vegetable garden. He planted green beans, peas, tomatoes, melons, cucumbers, squash, and berries, as well as oranges, avocados, grapefruit, tangerines, apricots, nectarines, plums, peaches, cherries, olives, and walnuts.

Explore the Huntington Gardens Today

Follow the Huntington's paths through sunshine and shade. Discover mysterious places and meet amusing garden friends. The lion dog guards an entrance to the Chinese garden. The lady scarecrow in the herb garden is always wearing a different outfit. The golden barrel cactus plants look like a group of creatures from a distant world, standing in formation.

5

The Japanese garden has koi fish that glitter in the sunshine as they swim under the bridges and around the pond. Near the entrance to the Japanese garden you will find two Queensland lace bark trees from Australia. In July the trees are filled with beautiful pink flowers.

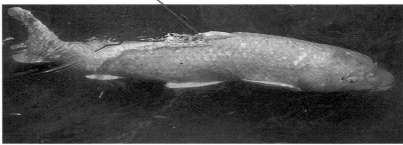

The Children's Garden: Play with Water, Walk in Fog

Enter the magical children's garden through the blue gate.

This large black crow watches over an exhibit that demonstrates magnetism. How does magnetism work? Look for various scientific principles hidden in the exhibits.

Have you ever heard of the four basic elements? What are they? Can you find them in the garden? Why do you see a rainbow in the garden when it isn't raining? Fog is made from what element? What does one of the exhibits teach you about fire?

Activity: Explore All of the Huntington Gardens

The gardens provide a kaleidoscope of learning experiences about plants and wildlife. This activity takes you through the gardens to learn about unusual plants.

You will need:
Notebook with blank pages
Colored pencils or pens
Map of the Huntington for visitors

1. On the first page of your notebook, write your name and the date and time of your visit. Take a few minutes to write your observations about the day: the season of the year, the weather, the temperature.

2. Write the name of each garden (listed around the kaleidoscope image at right) on the top of a blank page.

3. Begin your search by visiting the ombu tree in the jungle garden. On the jungle garden page, write "ombu tree." Then write the botanical name,* the country it comes from, the age of the tree, and other information to help you remember it. Draw a picture of the ombu tree. Do you see anything interesting nearby? Insects, birds, or anything unusual?

4. Now visit the other Huntington gardens, one by one, to find other plants or trees that interest you. You might want to look for: lotus flowers (lily ponds), a strawberry snowball tree (near the lily ponds), oak trees like the ones in Robin Hood's Sherwood Forest (big lawn near the entrance), boojum trees (desert garden), bamboo (Japanese garden), or golden barrel cactus (desert garden).

* Signs near many of the plants and trees give both their common names and their botanical names.

Wildlife you might meet along the way

Most of the Huntington's wildlife stays hidden when guests are visiting the grounds, but if you are quiet, you might see a hummingbird gathering nectar from bright red flowers in the desert garden. A lizard might be scurrying among the cactus.

In the spring, ducks nest and raise their young near the lily ponds. You might see a turtle or a frog. In the late afternoon in the Australian garden you may hear the "hoo-hoo, hoo-hoo" of a great horned owl from high overhead or off in the distance.

Great blue herons and great egrets stop by the pond in the Japanese garden when searching for food. Large orange fish called koi swim in the ponds.

Big handsome birds called red-shafted flickers dig in the bark of trees for insects. They and their close relatives, the wood-peckers, are common in the garden all year.

Look for California quail in the Shakespeare garden in spring and summer, and don't be surprised to see robins patrolling the lawns for worms. Robins are year-round residents.

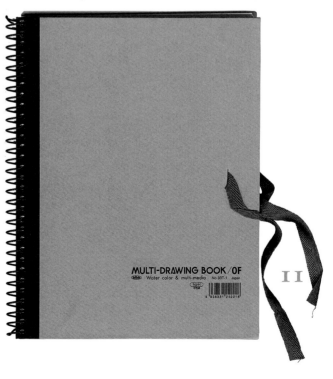

Explore the Botanical Conservatory

These children are learning what plants are up to in the botanical conservatory.

What makes a bog?   Count the insect corpses in a pitcher plant.   Look for a kaleidoscope in here.

Below: the outside of the botanical conservatory   Above: inside, a variety of leaves

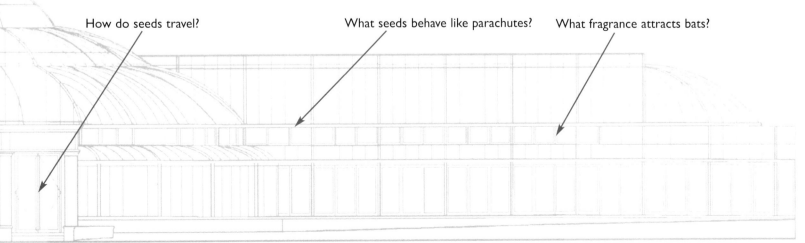

How do seeds travel?   What seeds behave like parachutes?   What fragrance attracts bats?

Activity: Go on a Seed Hunt

In the plant lab of the botanical conservatory are plastic bags displaying different kinds of seeds. Four of these bags are pictured here. All of the seeds (except for the pachypodium seeds) can easily be found around Southern California. You can substitute dandelion seeds for the pachypodium seeds. Corn seeds, which are plentiful in the autumn, might be found in a pet store. This is a good fall activity, since many plants complete their growing cycles as the hot summer comes to an end.

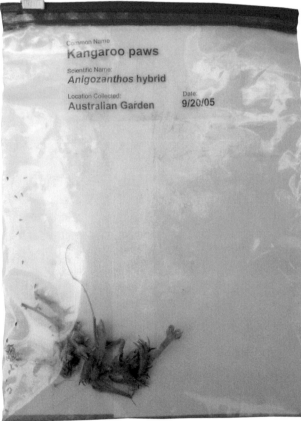

Kangaroo paw seeds

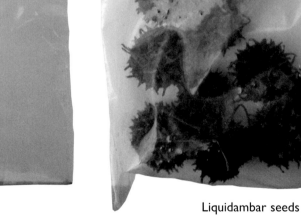

Liquidambar seeds

You will need:

Heavy-duty reclosable plastic bags, about 8 x 10 inches each
Clear labels, about 3 x 5 inches
Waterproof marking pen

Go on a hunt to find seeds like the ones shown below. Place only one kind of seed in each plastic bag and make a label with the name, date, and place you found it. You can get help identifying seeds at the botanical conservatory or a nursery.

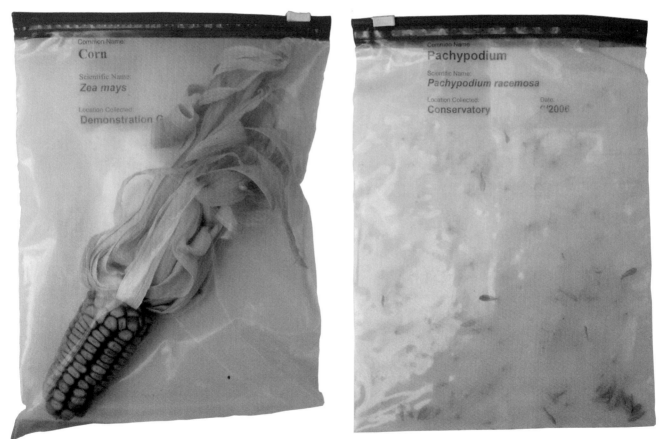

Corn seeds   Pachypodium seeds

How Do Seeds Travel?

Have you ever walked on a lawn and noticed a plant other than grass growing there? How do you think these plants—violets, dandelions, and oxalis are common Southern California lawn invaders—came to grow there if they weren't planted by gardeners?

In the plant lab area of the conservatory you can learn how seeds travel from place to place. Seeds of cotton and orchid plants are blown in the wind to new homes where, if growing conditions are right, they will sprout new plants. The seeds from a maple tree look like small helicopter blades. They twist and twirl in the autumn wind until they find a place to grow. Pine tree seeds travel in the same way. In the South Pacific seeds from coconut trees float in the water until they find a new home. Birds eat many kinds of fruit and their droppings spread fruit seeds. Some seeds—wisteria, for example—grow in pods until they dry out at the end of the summer. The warm autumn sun causes the pods to explode and scatter the seeds.

Seeds catch a ride on sheep wool.

Seeds catch a ride on coyote fur.

These seeds are found in Southern California. They are from a liquidambar tree, a pecan tree, an oak tree, wheat, a tulip magnolia tree, and a wisteria. Can you match the seeds with the plants they come from? Which ones would be relocated by birds? By squirrels and other animals? Which ones would catch a ride in animal fur or on a person's sock?

Seeds catch a ride on raccoon fur.

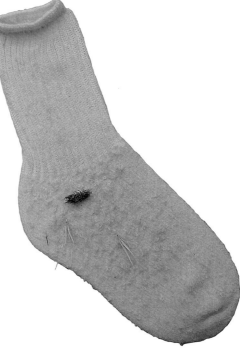

Seeds catch a ride on a sock.

Activity: Grow Plants from Seeds

You will need:

Package of seeds (see suggestions below)

Aluminum pie pan

Several paper towels

Three 12-inch (or larger) flowerpots filled with soil

To sprout a seed: Open the package and remove three seeds. Fold two paper towels in half and put them in the pie pan. Put the seeds on the paper towels and cover the pan with another damp paper towel. Put the pan in a warm place and pour a little water into it. Check twice a day to be sure that the paper towels are still damp. On the third day, carefully lift the top paper towel to check if the seeds have sprouted.

Place a sprouted seed, root end down, in each soil-filled flowerpot. Press a second, unsprouted seed into the soil a few inches from the sprouted seed. Put the pots outside and water daily if the weather is warm. In a few weeks, either seed—or both—will produce a plant. If you grow scarlet runner beans, the red flowers will turn into seedpods with beautiful bright-pink spotted beans inside. Sunflowers will be attractive to birds and squirrels, who will eat the seeds hidden in the center of the blossoms.

San Diego Museum of Natural History

BAJA CALIFORNIA, MEXICO

Sierra Juárez

Potentilla biennis Greene

Petals yellow.

Common in damp soil near natural pond 2 km
SE of San Faustino.

Near 32° 12 ′N, 116° 09½′W   Elevation ca. 1290 m.

Reid Moran 29649   28 June 1981

20

The Huntington's Herbarium

A herbarium is a collection of dried plants used for scientific study. The dried plants are called specimens because each one is an example of a certain kind of plant. For each specimen, like the one on the previous page, parts of plants that are useful in identifying it are dried under pressure and then mounted on paper to serve as a lasting record. The first herbariums were book-like volumes of dried medicinal plants, which were consulted by doctors.

Over time the collections have become larger. They are useful today not only to provide information about plants and where they come from but also to identify and name unfamiliar plants when they are discovered. Herbariums are also useful in settling disputes over the correct name of a plant. Today the oldest and largest herbarium in the world is in the Muséum National d'Histoire Naturelle in Paris, France. It was founded more than 200 years ago and contains over 8 million specimens. The Huntington's herbarium was created in 1964 and now has about 10,000 dried plant specimens from around the world. The majority are from Mexico, Central America, and South America.

```
HUNTINGTON BOTANICAL
GARDENS HERBARIUM

HNT    1337
```

This label shows the collection number for the plant to the left. In a large collection it is important to number the specimens.

Activity: Starting a Herbarium

You will need:
Plant suitable for drying (flax, asters, goldenrod, statice, Queen Anne's lace)
Two or more sheets of corrugated cardboard, about 15 x 20 inches
Two or more sheets of blotter paper or absorbent chipboard, about 15 x 20 inches
Newspaper
Heavy string
Lightweight white board or thick acid-free paper
White glue
Label for mounting

Gather a few plants suitable for drying. The plants listed above are often sold as part of mixed-flower bouquets. You may also find them growing in a yard. Gather the rest of the supplies together and spread them out on a clean, uncluttered workspace.

Place a piece of corrugated cardboard on the table. Lay a piece of blotter paper on top of the cardboard and then unfold a newspaper section, centering it on the blotter paper and cardboard as shown. Carefully lay a plant sample on the newspaper. Gently spread the plant out so it is lying flat, arranging it so you can see its parts. Fold the newspaper in half, covering the plant sample completely. Place the second piece of blotter paper on top and then put the second sheet of corrugated cardboard on top of the blotter paper.

You could repeat these steps with several plant specimens, sandwiching them between layers of newspaper, blotter paper, and cardboard. Tie the string around the outside layers, and if you like, place a brick or a heavy book on top of them. Air will travel through the corrugations of the cardboard, allowing the plants to dry. Don't open the cardboard sandwich for two weeks.

Flax blooms in July in Southern California.

22

Blotter paper or chipboard

Blotter paper or chipboard

Flax plant

Newspaper

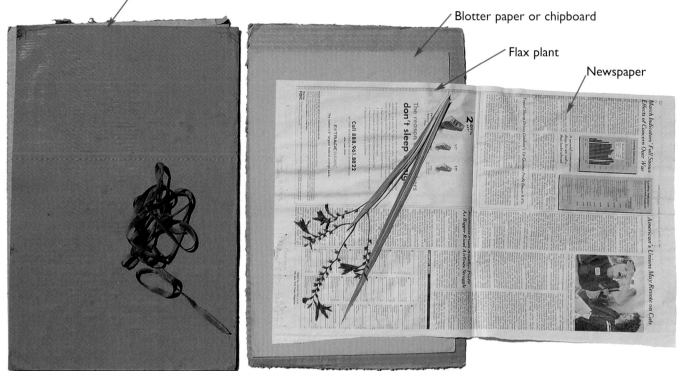

After the plants are dry, untie the cardboard sheets and remove the layers of blotter paper and newspaper. Carefully move the plant samples to the white board. Stick them in place with small amounts of white glue.

Your herbarium specimens will have scientific value if you follow these guidelines. Attach a label with your name, the date the plant was pressed, the botanical name of the plant (if you know it), and exactly where you found it. This information can prove invaluable, and you never know who will be using your dried plant specimens in a hundred years' time!

Corrugated cardboard tied with heavy string

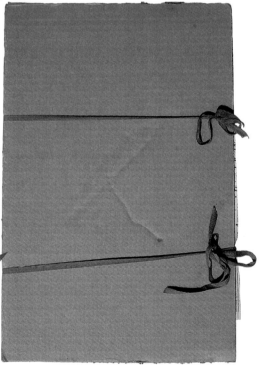

Building the Huntington Mansion

Even though Henry owned the San Marino Ranch, he lived in downtown Los Angeles. When he decided he wanted to live on the ranch, he hired an architect to draw up plans for a mansion to replace the house that was already there.

The new house was to be built in the popular Beaux-Arts style of architecture, which was taught at the famous École des Beaux-Arts (School of Fine Arts) in France. Beaux-Arts buildings are large and very formal in their appearance. The entrances are accented with heavy columns. Balustrades, decorative flower garlands, and square-cut crenelations also ornament the structure.

These are Ionic columns.　　Square-cut crenelations trim the building.

This is the top of an Ionic column.

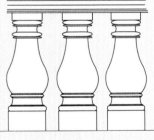

A baluster is a small column that supports a railing.

Here is a picture of the men who built Henry's Beaux-Arts mansion. How many can you count? Can you find a small dog in the picture? Can you find the flower garlands? Hint: look beside the Ionic columns.

Henry's mansion was constructed on the site of the existing house, which he said had the best view in all of Los Angeles. When the old house was torn down, the materials were not wasted; they were used to build houses for the ranch workers. A railroad track was laid to deliver heavy construction materials to the building site. Five very large trees had to be moved to new locations on the ranch.

Henry carefully watched over his new home as it was being built. He visited the construction site almost daily and talked with the workmen—he knew them all by name. Once or twice he even lent a hand when it was needed. The Los Angeles newspapers reported on the construction progress of the "palace." One reporter said of Henry, "He is enjoying the building of that house as no owner has before."

The Huntington mansion is almost 100 years old. It has recently been restored. New electrical wiring has replaced the aging, almost worn-out old wires, new plumbing was installed, and the rooms and the outside all have new coats of paint. This is a picture of the people who worked on the restoration. How many can you count? Can you find Ionic columns and crenelations in the picture?

A Beaux-Arts Mansion

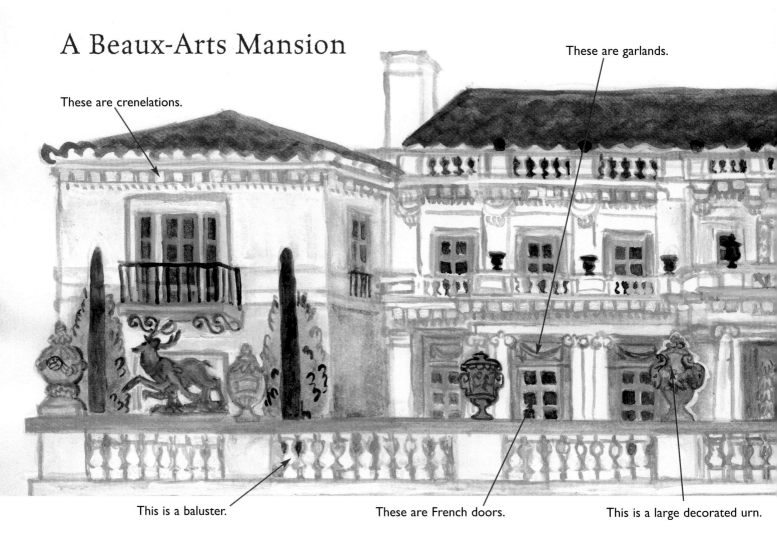

These are crenelations.

These are garlands.

This is a baluster.

These are French doors.

This is a large decorated urn.

This watercolor painting of the south side of the mansion as it looks today shows the details of Beaux-Arts architecture.

Balcony: a raised platform projecting from the side of a building

Baluster: a small column that supports a railing

Balustrade: a series of balusters

Column: an upright or vertical support of greater length than thickness (see "Ionic column")

Crenelations: square indentations along the edges of a building

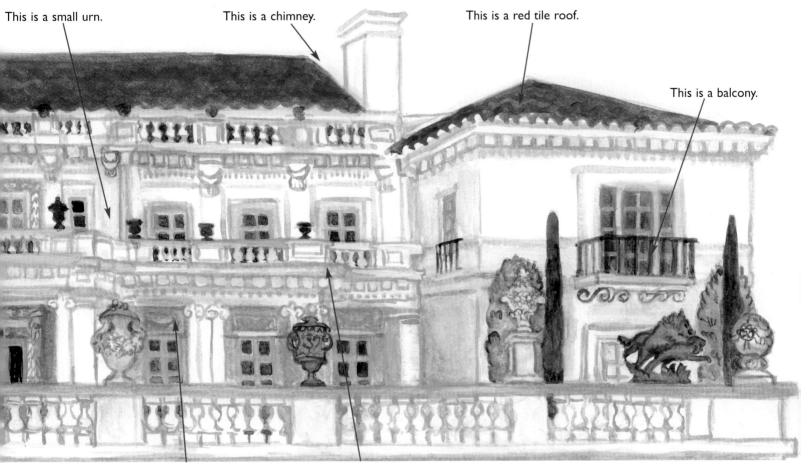

This is a small urn.

This is a chimney.

This is a red tile roof.

This is a balcony.

These are Ionic columns.

This is a terrace.

This watercolor picture was painted by Bunny Pierce Huffman.

French doors: a pair of doors opening onto a terrace

Garland: a string of flowers and leaves, often draped from one point to another

Ionic column: a style of classical Greek column that has symmetrical curlicues at the top (see the illustration on page 24)

Terrace: a large porch raised above the ground

Tile roof: a roof made from pieces of shaped clay

Urn: a container or vase that sits on a base or pedestal

Meet Arabella and Henry Huntington

In the early 1900s Arabella Huntington, widow of Henry's uncle, Collis, was one of the wealthiest women in the United States. She especially loved jewelry made with pearls. In this portrait she is wearing pearl earrings and a necklace that is made from six strands of luminous pearls.

Arabella was an art collector who filled her very large house on Fifth Avenue in New York with lovely things: fine linens, silver, crystal, china, furniture, jewelry, clothing, and paintings. The house, which had three attics and two basements, was big enough to hold everything she collected.

Arabella was fond of decorated objects that were made in France. This clock is an example of French decorative art. There is a portrait at the top. Whose picture might have been painted on a fancy clock? Can you find three angels on the front of the clock? Do you see any elements of French Beaux-Arts architecture?

Arabella loved to visit Europe, especially France. Once, when she was traveling with her son and daughter-in-law, they had six hundred pieces of luggage. How many people would have to travel with them to keep track of all that luggage?

28

Henry and Arabella were about the same age. They were close friends. She lived in New York City and he lived in California, but he often traveled east to visit her. Arabella encouraged and advised Henry about enlarging his own art collection. He welcomed her advice, but he only purchased paintings that he liked.

At first, Henry bought three well-known portraits. He enjoyed them so much that he purchased several more. He became an important collector of English portraits, and he often bought paintings of children. You will meet some of them when you turn the page.

Henry fell in love with Arabella, and they were married in 1913. She didn't like Southern California, but she lived part of every year in the Beaux-Arts mansion on the San Marino Ranch to please Henry. The Huntingtons had automobiles and a chauffeur to drive them wherever they wanted to go. Sometimes they traveled in their own private railroad car.

The Huntingtons were well-known members of the Southern California social and business communities. A railroad spike (below) was given as a favor at a dinner held to honor Henry's contributions to Southern California. You will learn more about Henry on page 57.

DINNER TO H. E. HUNTINGTON
HOTEL MARYLAND
PASADENA. OCT. 2. 1906

Children in the Huntington Art Collections

Jane Allnut (detail) by Sir Thomas Lawrence (1769–1830)

Master William Blair (detail) by Sir Henry Raeburn (1756–1853)

Look for paintings of children in the Huntington galleries. How many can you find? Many of these paintings were purchased by Henry. Others came to the Huntington after his death.

The children in the paintings lived long ago. Do you like the way they are dressed? Look for a pet in one of the paintings. Do you like the artists' choice of colors? Which painting do you like best? Tour guides and teachers will tell you more about when and where the children lived, what kind of clothing they wore, and what pastimes and games they enjoyed.

William Morris, Mary Cassatt, Thomas Gainsborough, Frederic Church, Thomas Lawrence,

Have you noticed that four of these children were painted by Sir Thomas Lawrence?

Thomas was a boy wonder. He was so clever with pencil and paper that people bought his drawings when he was only ten. As Thomas grew to manhood, people admired his good looks, his charming personality, and his skill as a portrait painter. He was elected to the Royal Academy—an honor reserved for the best English painters—at age twenty-five. This was an amazing accomplishment for such a young man.

Thomas Moran, John Singer Sargent, Charles and Henry Greene, Edward Hopper, Gilbert Stuart

Emily Anderson, Little Red Riding Hood (detail) by Sir Thomas Lawrence

Young Hobbinol and Ganderetta (detail) by Sir Thomas Lawrence

31

Meet Pinkie

In the late 1700s, a wealthy English family, the Barrett Moultons, lived on the island of Jamaica in the Caribbean Sea below the coast of south Florida. They owned land that produced rum and sugarcane, two of Jamaica's most important products.

Sarah Barrett Moulton, nicknamed "Pinkie," was born in Jamaica on March 22, 1783. She lived in a big house perched on top of a hill covered with cinnamon trees. It was no wonder the Barrett Moulton house was known as Cinnamon Hill. Imagine how pleasant Sarah's childhood was, spent in this warm tropical climate cooled by fresh ocean breezes scented with cinnamon.

At age twelve Sarah and her two younger brothers were sent to England to attend boarding school. The Barrett Moulton children traveled with their mother, their grandparents, and a tutor. It took six to eight weeks to sail from Jamaica to England—a long, cramped journey made worse by bad weather, worry about pirate attacks, and the threat of war between England and France.

The children arrived safely, but perhaps Sarah's health suffered on the long trip, for her grandmother, Judith Barrett, wrote about Sarah's persistent cough in several letters. When Judith returned to Jamaica she missed Sarah terribly. She wrote to a relative in England asking her to find a painter to make a fine picture of her dear granddaughter, and Thomas Lawrence was chosen to paint Sarah's portrait.

Look at Pinkie's portrait. The scene is a hilltop with a distant view and a dramatic cloudy sky. The wind is blowing. Pinkie is reaching to catch the ribbon on her bonnet. The background is out of focus, bringing attention to Pinkie's face and figure. Her face is painted in the finest detail. The painting sparkles with touches of color and light. The low horizon line puts Pinkie on the crest of a hill. The past is behind her. The future is ahead and out of our sight.

Pinkie's portrait was painted by Sir Thomas Lawrence.

33

Meet the Blue Boy

The young man who posed in a fancy blue costume for this portrait was Jonathan Buttall. His father was a friend of Thomas Gainsborough, the artist who painted the portrait. Jonathan's father was an "ironmonger," which means he sold hardware. Unlike Pinkie's family, the Buttall family was not wealthy. Pinkie's family hired an artist to paint her portrait, and they could afford to pay a high price. This was not true of Jonathan Buttall's family. It is not known exactly why Gainsborough chose to paint the "Blue Boy." He may have been challenged by an artist friend, or he might have wished to honor a painter he admired, Sir Anthony van Dyck. Perhaps Gainsborough painted the portrait of young Jonathan Buttall for his own enjoyment.

One hundred years ago, Gainsborough's "Blue Boy" was considered to be the finest of all English portraits. Henry Huntington admired the painting and wanted to buy it for his collection. However, the "Blue Boy" belonged to another collector and was not for sale—but Henry was patient. Eventually, he asked his art dealer to offer the owner a very large sum of money for the painting. His offer was accepted. It was a record price—the highest price ever paid for a painting at that time. Henry hung it in the large drawing room of his mansion. After he died it was moved to the house's main gallery, where you can see it when you visit.

Look at the Blue Boy's portrait. In the background there is a stormy sky and trees that appear to be blowing in the wind. Notice that the sky and the trees are not painted in the same detail as the figure of the boy. In fact, the most noticeable elements in the painting—other than the boy's finely painted face—are his fancy blue clothing and feather-trimmed hat. Even his pants and shoes are trimmed with large blue bows. This style of clothing is called "van Dyck dress" after the artist Sir Anthony van Dyck, who often painted subjects costumed in a similar fashion.

The Blue Boy's portrait was painted by Thomas Gainsborough.

Who Works in the Art Galleries?

Françoise Holding a Little Dog, a drawing by Mary Cassatt

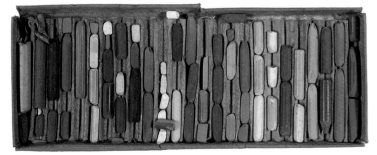

* Such as cloth, woven fabrics, rugs
** Such as china, dishes, silver, clocks

Art curators are in charge of the Huntington's art galleries. They are experts in English and American paintings, sculptures, furniture, textiles,* and decorative objects.** They share information about these works of art by writing books and articles, teaching classes, giving talks and lectures, and leading gallery tours.

There are two kinds of exhibits at most art museums. Permanent exhibits include the most important paintings, and they are on display almost all the time. The Huntington's most famous paintings that are on permanent display are *Pinkie* and *The Blue Boy*. Curators choose the artwork that will be displayed in changing exhibits, which are usually installed in special rooms for only a short period of time and sometimes include works loaned by other museums. Exhibit designers assist the curators in preparing changing exhibits. Preparators help by framing and hanging the works of art for an exhibit. Guards carefully watch over the galleries and also answer questions. You will see tour guides, or docents, leading schoolchildren and other groups and telling interesting stories about the Huntington and its works of art. When you visit, be on your best behavior, follow the rules, and have a wonderful time!

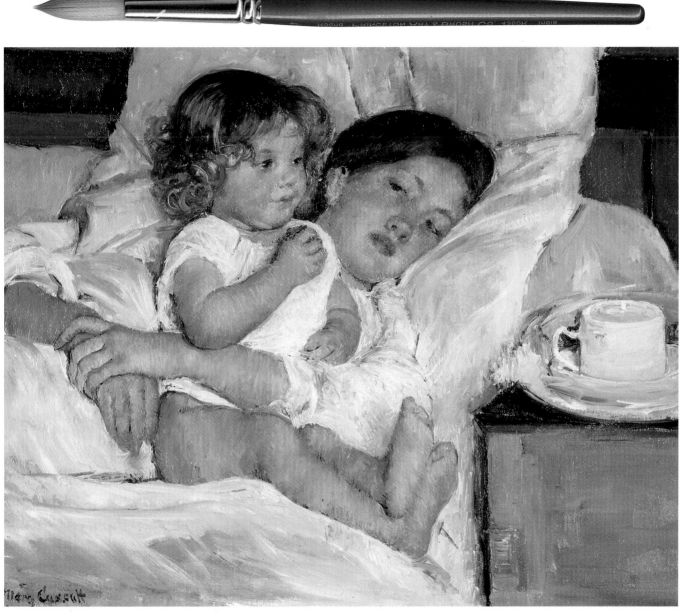

Breakfast in Bed, a painting by Mary Cassatt, is on permanent exhibit in the Scott Gallery. Mary Cassatt lived from 1844 to 1926. She grew up near Pittsburgh, Pennsylvania, and later lived and worked in Paris, France.

Do you see a difference between the surface texture of the drawing to the left and the surface texture of the painting above? What is the reason for the different textures?

Activity: Photograph or Draw a Portrait

You have just looked at some portraits of children. A portrait is an artist's drawing, painting, or photograph of a person or an animal. The portrait shows what the person or animal looks like, and it may also give clues to their personality. Portraits are usually created while the artist is looking at the real person rather than working from their memory or imagination.

In this activity you are the portrait artist, and you will compose a portrait of a friend and add clues to the picture. Dress your friend up in a costume and add objects to the picture that mean something to him or her.

You will need:
Camera with a flash
Chair carefully placed in a yard or park
Costume and objects

Decide what you want the viewers of the portrait to learn about your friend—make a list. Gather together the costume and objects you will need to illustrate the items on the list. Set a chair outside in a place with a pleasing background of leaves or plants. Seat your friend on the chair and arrange the objects nearby. Take about six different pictures in the early morning or late afternoon to avoid strong sunlight. Print the pictures and check your results. If you are not happy, try again. Artists often spend long hours improving their work. Keep trying until you are pleased with the results. If you like, make a frame for your favorite portrait.

Who Am I?

Clue 1: Captured soldiers are marching in the background.

Clue 2: Captured enemy flags are on the ground.

Clue 3: This is the head of the officer's horse.

Clue 4: The blue sash crossing his chest shows that he is a commander in chief.

Clue 5: The officer's hand is resting on an old-style military cannon.

When artists paint portraits, they decide what clues to put in the painting. The clues give us information about the person. The red arrows point to clues about the identity of the man in this painting. Guess who he is and then visit the Scott Gallery to see if you are right.

Write a Story About a Landscape Painting

Landscape paintings show a view of the outdoors. The large landscape paintings in the Huntington galleries can take you on a trip to visit places far away and long ago. *Vesuvius from Portici* pictures the eruption of Mt. Vesuvius in the year 79—1,700 years before English artist Joseph Wright worked on the painting (from 1774 until 1776). Wright painted from his imagination. American artist Edward Hopper painted *The Long Leg* in "real time," showing the seascape as it appeared about 1935, when he worked on the painting.

In both paintings, color plays an important role in how we react to the landscape. In *Vesuvius from Portici* the painter has used oranges and reds, colors that make us feel hot, to show how an explosion of burning lava looks and feels. The cool blue colors in *The Long Leg* help us imagine how peaceful it feels to look out over the sea on a sunny day. Do you like the way these two paintings look together? Orange and blue are called complementary colors because they are directly across the color wheel from each other, as shown on the next page. They make us think of opposite temperatures—warm and cool.

Write a short story about one of the paintings, using color to set the mood for your story. Before you begin writing, ask yourself the following questions.

1. What is happening in the painting?
2. Did the artist paint from imagination or real life?
3. Does the main color in the painting make you feel warm or cool, happy or sad, peaceful or worried?

40

orange

blue

This is a color wheel showing the three primary colors—red, yellow, blue—and the three secondary colors—orange, green, violet. The six colors of the color wheel are always arranged in this order.

Vesuvius from Portici was painted by English artist Joseph Wright of Derby. He lived from 1734 to 1797.

The bright orange colors in Vesuvius from Portici complement the color blue.

This is a painting by American artist Edward Hopper, who lived from 1882 to 1967. It is called The Long Leg.

The blue colors in this painting complement the color orange.

The Beginning of the Huntington Library

When Henry was a young man, he loved to read and learn from books. As he grew older he began to collect books—an amazing number of books. He lived at a private club when he was in New York City, and that is where he stored his book collection. Friends who visited him said, "Every chair and table, as well as the floor beneath his bed, was covered not only with books and manuscripts but also a fine layer of dust because he didn't want his prized possessions damaged by careless cleaning."

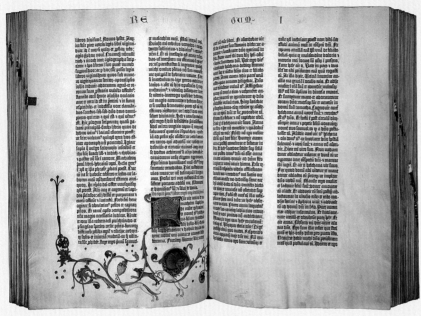

The Huntington Library's Gutenberg Bible

A collection of books is called a library. Henry's library was called the "library of libraries" after he purchased several libraries from other book collectors. Henry was a multimillionaire, so he could buy as many books as he wanted. One of these books was a decorated copy of the Gutenberg Bible. Gutenberg Bibles were the first books printed in Europe on a printing press. They are very rare: there are only forty-eight left in the world today. Henry paid an enormous price—$50,000 for his Bible—more than any book collector had ever paid for a book in the early twentieth century. You can see this Bible on display in the library exhibition hall.

Henry collected hundreds of thousands of books, letters, diaries, maps, photographs, and documents for his library. In 1921 he had a large library building constructed on his San Marino ranch near his new Beaux-Arts mansion. When it was finished, Henry's books were carefully packed and moved from New York to San Marino.

Our Founding Fathers at the Huntington Library

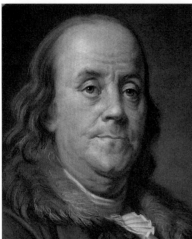

The millions of items in the Huntington Library are studied by historians and researchers. There is also a library exhibition room as well as occasional special exhibits of objects from the library open to the public.

The paintings and manuscripts illustrated here are part of the American history collection, which includes portraits of George Washington, Benjamin Franklin, and Abraham Lincoln, as well as papers and other objects once written or owned by important men and women from our country's history. Do you recognize the people in the portraits?

At the top of the next page Benjamin Franklin's autobiography is shown. An autobiography is the story that a person writes about their own life. Franklin wanted to share his memories and wisdom with his son, and wrote the book as if speaking to him. Below Franklin's autobiography is a letter written by Abraham Lincoln when he was president.

These are only a few of the many rare and wonderful items that are housed in the library.

Shakespeare, Abraham Lincoln, Benjamin Franklin, George Washington, Audubon, Jack Londo

Franklin's "Thirteen Virtues" manuscript (top), left page:

1. Temperance.
Eat not to Dulness
Drink not to Elevation.

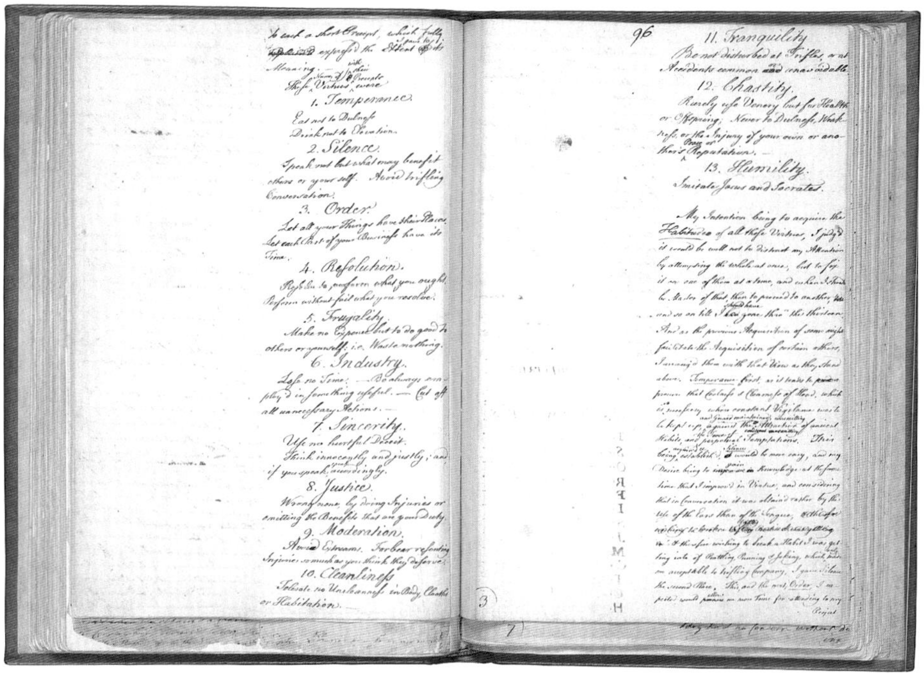

2. Silence.
Speak not but what may benefit
others or your self. Avoid trifling
Conversation.

3. Order.
Let all your Things have their Places
let each Part of your Business have its
Time.

4. Resolution.
Resolve to perform what you ought
Perform without fail what you resolve.

5. Frugality.
Make no Expense but to do good to
others or yourself; ie. Waste nothing.

6. Industry.
Lose no Time. Be always em-
ploy'd in something useful. Cut off
all unnecessary Actions.

7. Sincerity.
Use no hurtful Deceit
Think innocently and justly; and
if you speak, speak accordingly.

8. Justice.
Wrong none by doing Injuries or
omitting the Benefits that are your Duty.

9. Moderation.
Avoid Extreams. Forbear resenting
Injuries so much as you think they deserve.

10. Cleanliness.
Tolerate no Uncleanness in Body, Cloaths
or Habitation.

96

11. Tranquility
Be not disturbed at Trifles, or at
Accidents common and unavoidable.

12. Chastity.
Rarely use Venery but for Health
or Offspring, Never to Dulness, Weak-
ness, or the Injury of your own or another's Peace or Reputation.

13. Humility.
Imitate Jesus and Socrates.

Handwritten notebook (bottom), left page:

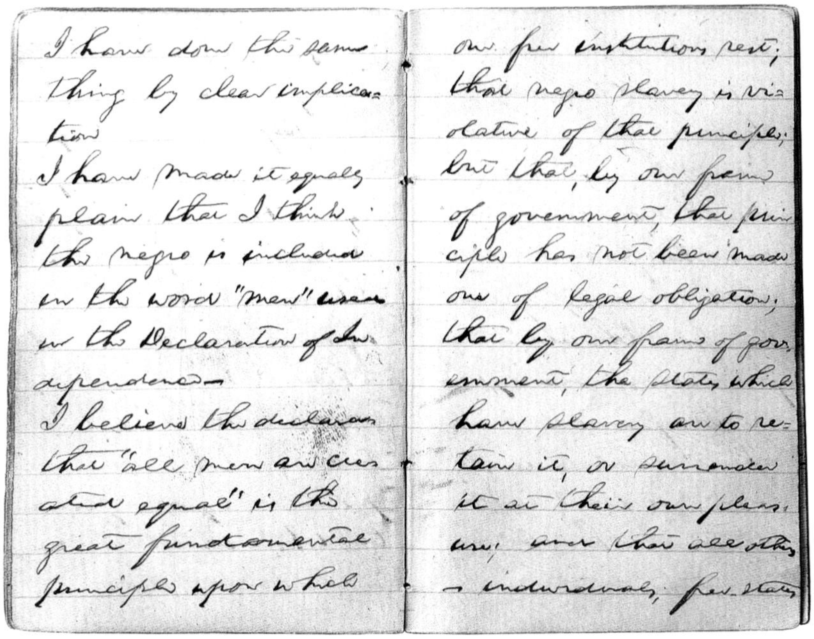

I have done the same
thing by clear implica-
tion
I have made it equally
plain that I think
the negro is included
in the word "men" used
in the Declaration of In-
dependence—
I believe the declaration
that "all men are cre-
ated equal" is the
great fundamental
principle upon which

our free institutions rest;
that negro slavery is vi-
olative of that principle;
but that, by our frame
of government, that prin-
ciple has not been made
one of legal obligation;
that by our frame of gov-
ernment, the states which
have slavery are to re-
tain it, or surrender
it at their own pleas-
ure; and that all other
individuals, free states

Working Inside the Huntington Library

Have any of your schoolbooks come apart at the binding or spine? Do the covers look beaten up because they have been used so much? Your schoolbooks aren't very old. Does this make you wonder about the really old books in the Huntington Library? Some of the millions of valuable books and objects in the library are 500 to 1,000 years old. They need special care. Sometimes they need to be taken apart and carefully rebound.

The woman in the photo—a book conservator—is repairing an old book. She is using a wooden frame to carefully sew together the pages of a book that was printed in 1493. When she finishes sewing she will use the tools on the next page to make a new binding and cover for the book. Rebinding books is a slow and difficult process. It is only one of the important jobs carried out by the library's staff.

Curators teach about the books and manuscripts (letters and diaries that are written by hand) by organizing exhibits, writing books and articles, giving lectures, teaching classes, and answering questions from students. Other people who work in the library are librarians and photographers. Librarians organize books and manuscripts in a scientific way to help researchers find the materials and information they need. Photographers take pictures of many things in the library, for researchers, authors, and other museums all over the world.

Some of the old books in the library were originally written for children, such as *A Visit from St. Nicholas.* Photographers helped re-create the book in a new form that shows its beautiful illustrations. You can buy a copy in the bookstore.

The book conservator is sewing a book, Liber Chronicarum, a world history that was published in 1493.

Book conservators use many interesting tools when they repair very old books. Here are some of them. Can you find a brush, sewing thread, and a hammer?

What Is a Collection?

A collection is a set of objects that have something in common. A collection can be made up of any kind of object: books by a favorite author, seashells, handmade nutcrackers, baseball hats, and so on. All that is necessary to make a collection is a group of objects that share something similar.

For example, a woman named Diana Korzenik was interested in how American children have learned about art. She collected more than 1,500 objects: books for art teachers, drawing and painting books for children, and samples of children's art supplies. Not all of the objects in her collection are in perfect condition—while some have never been used, others are quite worn. The condition of the objects was not as important as collecting them in order to give a picture of how art was taught to American children long ago.

Diana Korzenik gave her collection to the Huntington Library so it could be used by researchers who want to learn how art was taught to children. The pictures on these pages show different objects in the Korzenik collection.

A painting book

48

A box of colored chalk

A box of tempera paints

Dixon's Eldorado, the master drawing pencil, is made in 17 leads, ranging from 6B to 9H. The Dixon Visigrade (copyrighted) system of stamping the degree of hardness three times on each pencil——once on every other panel——enables the draftsman working with several degrees of hardness to pick out the degree he wishes at a glance. Architects, engin...

Crayonex
Sixteen Colors
THE PRANG COMPANY.
NewYork Chicago Boston Atlanta Dallas

7 KEYS TO ART

Boxes of crayons

A box of drawing pencils

49

Activity: Start a Collection

A collector gathers objects that are related to each other. The collection can include both new and used items. Sometimes the older items in a collection might be more valuable than newer ones. Baseball card collectors know that the most valuable baseball card is one from 1909 picturing Honus Wagner. One of these cards sold on eBay for more than one million dollars in 2000. And book collectors know that old books are sometimes more valuable than new books.

Collecting objects is fun. You can discover interesting objects in a closet or attic in your home. You can trade objects with friends who are interested in the same thing. You can hunt for new additions to your collection at garage sales, flea markets, rummage sales, junk stores, antique stores, or auctions. Putting together a collection can be competitive, absorbing, challenging, informative, and most of all, fun.

You will need:
Objects for your collection
A safe place to store your collection—a box or drawer will do
3-x-5-inch cards

Item I collected:

Date I bought it:
or
It was a gift from:

It was purchased: New   Used   (circle one)

It cost me: $

My notes: (write more on the other side)

When you have decided what you are going to collect, learn more about it from library books or by searching the Internet. You will find information from experts who will tell you more about the items you want to collect. It is important to keep records of the items in your collection. As you add new items, record information about them on index cards, one for each item.

50

If you decide to collect kaleidoscopes, you might want to join the Brewster Kaleidoscope Society (www.brewstersociety.com).

Activity: Organize a Family Photo Collection

In museums and libraries photography collections are stored in acid-free envelopes and boxes to protect the photos from being damaged by the harmful chemicals in some paper products. The photos are also organized according to a plan. This makes them easier to find and use. This activity shows how to organize your family photos so that everyone can enjoy them. Photos stored at home should also be placed in acid-free envelopes to keep them from being damaged and torn and to preserve them for family members in the future.

You will need:

An adult to help you

Acid-free file folders or plastic sleeves

An archival storage box

Press-on labels

Large index cards for dividers

Cotton gloves to protect photos from fingerprints

Clean table with adequate workspace

Archival supplies can be purchased at camera stores.

52

Place your photo collection on the table and put on the cotton gloves. Sort the photos into categories. Write the name of each category at the top of an index card. You can sort the photos by year, by family member, or by event. Some categories might be holiday photos, vacation photos, baby photos, school photos, birthday parties, and hiking trips.

Slip each photo into an envelope or plastic sleeve. Never write directly on a photo, even on the back, because the writing may leave a permanent trace. Identify who is in the picture and when and where it was taken. You may need help from a family member, especially if you have a lot of photos. Write the information on a press-on label and stick the label onto the photo sleeve. Sort the photos by category, place them in the storage box, and use the index cards as dividers between categories.

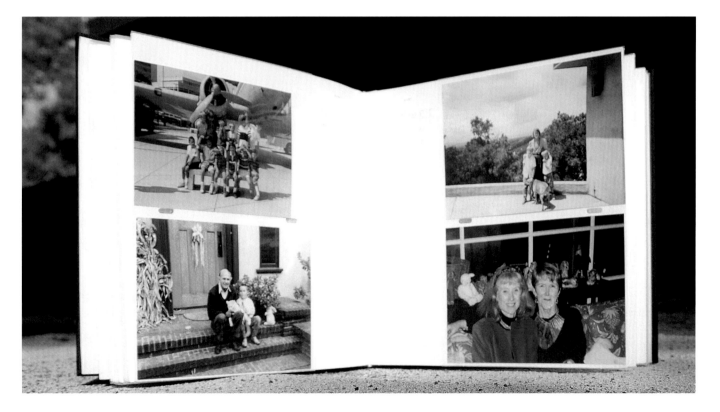

Activity: Make Your Own Bookplate

Bookplates are personalized labels used by book owners to identify their books. Pasting a label on the inside front cover of a book is a tradition that has been practiced almost as long as there have been printed books.

The first books were very valuable. They were produced entirely by hand and most of them were used for worship or prayer. These books took a long time—sometimes years—to make, and the materials used to make them were scarce. They were sometimes chained to a desk or shelf so that people wouldn't steal them. Even when there were more books, produced with a printing press rather than by hand, they were at first too expensive for most people to afford.

A book owner's bookplate had a custom design with the owner's name as well as a picture, a saying, or sometimes a poem. One old bookplate exclaimed, "Ho, there! Take me back to my master." The Latin phrase "Ex Libris" was traditionally included. "Ex Libris" means "from the books of." Failing to return a book could get you into serious trouble. Another bookplate had this threatening poem:

> Steal not this book my honest friend,
> For fear the gallows will be your end.
> Up the ladder and down the rope,
> There you'll hang until you choke.
> Then I'll come along and say,
> "Where's that book you stole away?"

Poem from The Outlook, December 6, 1902

Have you ever loaned a book that wasn't returned? Or lost a book that was important to you? Making a bookplate of your own can help you keep track of your books.

You will need:
White acid-free 100% cotton paper
Scissors
Ruler
Wheat-based glue
Pencils and marking pens

Special paper and glue can be purchased at an art-supply store.

Draw several 4-x-5-inch rectangles on the paper. You may be able to draw more than one on a sheet. Sketch out some designs for your bookplate until you find one that pleases you.

The design should be very simple. Remember to include your name and, if you like, "Ex Libris."

When you have made a design that you like, you can make several copies by photocopying it or by scanning it into a computer and then printing it. (Remember to use acid-free paper when you make the photocopies or printouts. Other types of paper may contain chemicals that could damage your books.)

Visit http://www.myhomelibrary.org to learn more about bookplates and to see some bookplates that were made by some of your favorite illustrators. Instead of creating your own design, you may want to print out the ones you like from the website, and then decorate and paste them on the inside covers of your books.

Henry Huntington when he was eight years old

Henry Huntington's Childhood

Henry Huntington was born in 1850—the exact middle of the nineteenth century. His family lived in Oneonta, a very small town in New York. The biggest yearly event was the day a traveling circus arrived in town, set up tents, and performed on the Huntington property.

The Huntingtons owned a general store in town and farms in the countryside. Oneonta was a pleasant place for children. It was a quiet country town with a main street, several stores, two hotels, and a two-room schoolhouse. If you took a stroll on a summer evening you might hear a brass band practicing above a store, people singing and playing instruments in their front parlors, or the Huntingtons reading books to their children.

In the summer the Huntington children walked the family cows to pasture and then spent the day swimming in a pond or playing hide-and-seek among fresh bales of hay. In the cold, snowy winter the children had to wear warm clothes and heavy woolen scarves and mittens when they sledded down snow-covered hillsides or ice-skated on frozen ponds. When the snow melted in the spring, they searched the woods and fields for wildflowers.

On frosty fall days Henry and his brothers hunted for chestnut trees in the fields around Oneonta. They competed with the local squirrels to find the best chestnuts to take home to their mother.

Later in Henry's life, when he lived in Southern California, he was interested in the squirrels he saw at Mt. Lowe, above Pasadena. He brought a pair of mountain squirrels back to his ranch and greatly increased the squirrel population in the San Gabriel Valley.

57

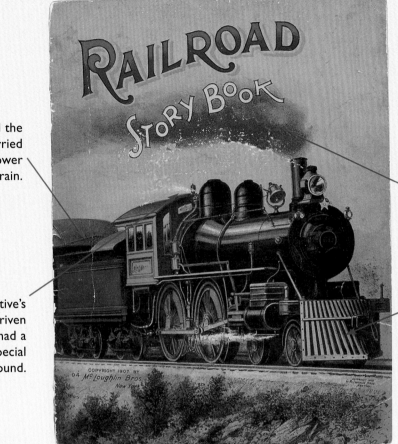

The car behind the locomotive carried coal to power the train.

Steam hissed from the steam-powered locomotive.

The locomotive's steam-driven whistle had a very special sound.

This piece of metal, called a cowcatcher, cleared the tracks of obstructions in front of the engine.

The steam train that arrived in Oneonta looked something like this. You can imagine the hiss of the steam from the engine and the throaty sound of the whistle.

When Henry was a boy, travel was slow—on foot, on horseback, by horse-pulled wagons, in carriages, and in commercial stagecoaches. The most modern form of travel, the New York Central passenger train, didn't run through town. This changed when the first passenger train arrived in Oneonta on August 29, 1865. Country folks traveled from nearby towns to witness the great event. Henry's younger brother Willard was nine years old, and he later said that the arrival of the train caused so much excitement among the small boys that they never forgot it. Trains became the main occupation of Oneonta boys: watching for trains, learning the names of the locomotives, and for the lucky, sitting with an engineer in the cab of a locomotive.

58

Working on the Railroad

The Huntington family—brothers, sisters, uncles, aunts, cousins, nieces, and nephews—was very close. It is not surprising that Henry worked for his father's successful older brother, Collis. Collis Huntington and his three partners, Leland Stanford (founder of Stanford University in Northern California), Charles Crocker, and Mark Hopkins, were in the railroad business. They owned the Southern Pacific Railroad.

Henry visited Southern California for the first time in 1892, when he was traveling with Uncle Collis on business. They stayed overnight with James Shorb, one of the earliest landowners in the San Gabriel Valley. Charmed by the beauty of the Shorb Ranch and the spectacular views of the surrounding countryside and mountains, Henry commented, "It was the prettiest place I had ever seen."

California Poppies, by Benjamin Brown, courtesy of the Pasadena Museum of History

This painting by Pasadena artist Benjamin Brown shows the San Gabriel Valley as Henry knew it.

Tourists Stream into Sunny Southern California

San Francisco was larger than Los Angeles in 1900. Los Angeles was spacious—many times bigger in area than San Francisco—but the population was much smaller. Businessmen who wanted to attract more visitors to their city formed the Los Angeles Board of Trade. Yearly winter attractions such as citrus festivals, the New Year's Day Rose Parade and Rose Bowl football game, an annual chariot race, and the springtime Los Angeles Festival of Flowers were created to attract tourists.

The advantages of the sunny and warm Southern California climate were advertised all around the country and the world. Los Angeles is a paradise—"an agreeable climate with an abundance of sunshine and fresh air to be enjoyed at an ocean beach, in the scenic mountains, or at the many resort hotels found on the fertile valleys." Southern California had plenty of open space. Newcomers needed houses, and they caused a building boom. Vacant city streets became lined with charming houses.

PASADENA, CALIFORNIA

Tourists enjoyed Southern California's warm winter weather. Here they are watching chariot races once held on New Year's Day.

. . . And So Does Henry Huntington

Collis Huntington died unexpectedly in 1900, and Henry inherited about $9 million—one-third of his uncle's estate—the equivalent of about $223 million today. Henry's own money that he had saved and invested was added to his inheritance and made him a very wealthy man. He could have retired, but his ambition was to follow in his uncle's footsteps. He hoped to replace his uncle as president of the Southern Pacific.

Although Henry was an excellent choice for president of the Southern Pacific Company, he was not elected, but this news did not slow him down. He decided to achieve success on his own in Los Angeles, the area that had attracted him for more than eight years. He was bursting with energy when he arrived in Los Angeles. More than any other local businessman, Henry Huntington believed in the future of the city of Los Angeles, and he was willing to risk his own fortune to promote and develop the city he loved.

Spring St. looking South from Franklin, Los Angeles, Cal.

On this postcard sent to a friend many years ago someone named Harry wrote, "L.A. isn't much of a town"—that was before Henry Huntington's arrival.

Spring Street in downtown Los Angeles in 1900. Transportation was by trolley, bicycle, horse, and horse-pulled buggy, or by foot. There were few automobiles.

Trolley Man

Streetcars pulled by teams of horses provided the first public transportation in Los Angeles. These streetcars were soon replaced by "horseless" trolleys powered by electricity. Public transportation was a promising new business opportunity in a growing city, and many small companies laid tracks and purchased electric trolley cars. Each company owned their own routes, created their own schedules, and charged their own fares. This created a tremendous problem for passengers who wanted to transfer from one trolley line to another.

Henry Huntington, "the Trolley Man," recognized the problem and had an excellent solution. He bought many of the small Los Angeles trolley companies and grouped them together into one system. His trolley system was called the Pacific Electric, or P.E. The "Red Cars" of the P.E. connected Los Angeles with surrounding towns and cities.

In this old picture of downtown Los Angeles, a full moon and the lights of the Los Angeles Railway's cars brighten up a night scene.

Henry's vision for Southern California included buying large areas of vacant land and dividing it into building lots and providing utilities—electricity, water, natural gas—to growing towns. The areas of Southern California developed by Henry were connected by the P.E. trolley service.

This brochure advertised four different sightseeing trolley trips around Southern California. The Red or Balloon Trip ran from Los Angeles to Redondo Beach to Venice to Santa Monica; the Blue or Old Mission Trip ran from Los Angeles to Alhambra or Pasadena or Glendora; the Yellow or Triangle Trip ran from Los Angeles to Santa Ana to Long Beach; and the Green or Mt. Lowe Trip ran from Los Angeles to Mt. Lowe, above Pasadena. You can see a map from the inside of this brochure on pages 66 and 67. All of the P.E. stops are named on the map. Did the P.E. stop near where you live?

63

Henry Huntington and His Electric Trolleys Roll Through Southern California

In fifteen years Henry Huntington shaped the city of Los Angeles. Follow his tracks from 1898 to 1910 to learn how he did it.

JANUARY, 1907

P.E. MAGAZINE

PACIFIC ELECTRIC BUILDING, LOS ANGELES
Showing Train Entrance to Station of P. E. and L. A. Inter-Urban Railways

COPYRIGHTED 1907 BY
THE P. E. PUBLISHING CO.
PACIFIC ELECTRIC BUILDING
LOS ANGELES, CAL.

PRICE 10 CENTS

To the left is the cover of an issue of "P. E. Magazine." Why is there an electric bolt in the logo?

To the right is Car #500. It still runs a short distance in San Pedro. You can catch a ride on it at the Ports of Call Station. Can you find San Pedro on the map on page 66?

1898 Henry buys LARY, the Los Angeles Railway. LARY's green trolleys run in downtown Los Angeles. Henry is living in San Francisco.

1901 Henry purchases several existing trolley companies (including the Los Angeles & Pasadena Railway and the Mt. Lowe Railway), consolidates them to form the Pacific Electric Railway (P.E.), and makes plans to extend service to new towns including Long Beach, Redlands, and Riverside.

1902 Henry moves to Los Angeles. When P.E. tracks are extended to Alhambra and Long Beach, land values double in Long Beach. Henry founds a real estate development company and an electric company.

Car #401, stopping in Monrovia to pick up passengers about 100 years ago

1903 P.E. tracks are extended to Monrovia and Whittier. There are now 170 miles of P.E. tracks.

1904 P.E. tracks are extended to Huntington Beach and Newport Beach. A new P.E. office building is completed in downtown Los Angeles. It is the largest office building west of Chicago.

1905 Henry buys the Los Angeles and Redondo Railway and opens a real estate sales company in Redondo Beach.

1906 Henry opens a new P.E. line to Pasadena, Sierra Madre, and Eagle Rock.

1907 P.E. tracks reach Covina and Glendora. Henry forms a water company to provide water to his real estate developments.

1908 Henry extends P.E. tracks to La Habra and makes connections between existing routes.

1909 Henry builds the largest indoor swimming center in the world in Redondo Beach.

1910 The Southern Pacific takes over ownership of the P.E. and Henry retires. Henry helps organize the world's first air show in Los Angeles.

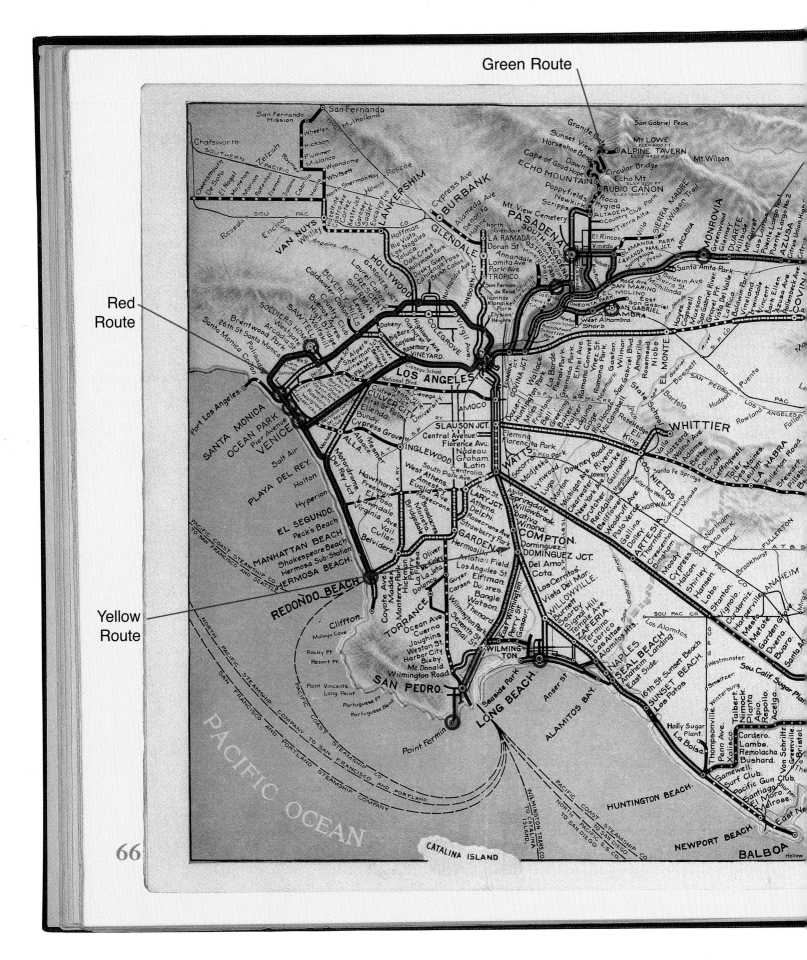

Green Route

Red
Route

Yellow
Route

66

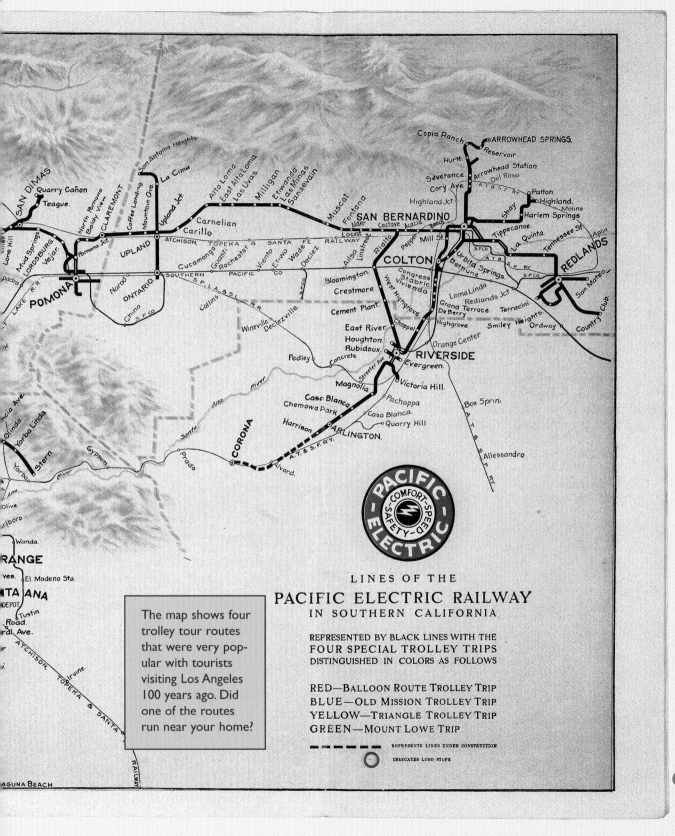

The map shows four trolley tour routes that were very popular with tourists visiting Los Angeles 100 years ago. Did one of the routes run near your home?

PACIFIC ELECTRIC
COMFORT - SPEED - SAFETY

LINES OF THE

PACIFIC ELECTRIC RAILWAY
IN SOUTHERN CALIFORNIA

REPRESENTED BY BLACK LINES WITH THE
FOUR SPECIAL TROLLEY TRIPS
DISTINGUISHED IN COLORS AS FOLLOWS

RED—BALLOON ROUTE TROLLEY TRIP
BLUE—OLD MISSION TROLLEY TRIP
YELLOW—TRIANGLE TROLLEY TRIP
GREEN—MOUNT LOWE TRIP

▪▪▪▪ REPRESENTS LINES UNDER CONSTRUCTION
◎ INDICATES LONG STOPS

67

Henry Retires

When Henry sold the Pacific Electric Company and retired, he had more time to spend with his wife, Arabella. The Huntingtons liked to travel. They traveled in their own private railroad car back and forth between New York and California. They traveled to Europe on luxury steamships. In California they traveled in Henry's private trolley car to downtown Los Angeles, and they sometimes packed a picnic and had their chauffeur drive them to a place near the beach with a beautiful view.

Daily life was restful and very genteel on the Huntington estate. Henry spent his days overseeing his gardens and his collections. Arabella collected art, visited with friends, and enjoyed her pets. Every night the Huntingtons dressed in their best formal clothes and ate dinner in the mansion's large dining room—even when they had no guests. After dinner they went upstairs and played card games before going to bed. It was a wonderful life at a time long ago, when life was less busy.

Turn the page to learn more about the contributions Henry Huntington made to Los Angeles and Southern California.

This is Henry's 1913 Lozier automobile.

Activity: Automobile Salad

(adapted from *Los Angeles Times Cookbook #2*, 1905)

One hundred years ago, if your family was lucky enough to own an automobile, you might have driven to the country on Sunday afternoon to enjoy a picnic that included an automobile salad.

You will need the help of an adult to make this salad.

Dressing Ingredients	Salad Ingredients
1 egg, beaten	4 tomatoes, chopped
4 tablespoons white wine vinegar	4 stalks of celery, chopped
1 teaspoon butter	2 heads of lettuce, torn
1/2 teaspoon dry mustard	1/2 cup pitted green olives
1/2 teaspoon salt	
1/4 teaspoon pepper	
2 tablespoons deviled ham or ham spread	
Light whipping cream to thin dressing	

Decorate the salad bowl with nasturtium flowers and leaves, if they are in season.

To make the dressing:

Fill the bottom of a double boiler with water and bring it to a gentle boil. Put the beaten egg in the double-boiler top and place it over the gently boiling water. Use a microwave to heat the white vinegar and stir the hot vinegar into the egg. Stir the egg and vinegar mixture constantly until it thickens. This will happen very quickly. Remove from the stove and stir in the butter, mustard, salt, pepper, and ham. Add cream to thin the dressing. Toss the salad ingredients with the dressing.

Below: A flyer for a bathhouse and swimming pool in Redondo Beach, built by Henry for public use

Upper right: The Huntington Hotel in Pasadena

Middle right: A hot-air balloon flies over the Huntington estate, shown in the distance

Lower right: A postcard from the first air show ever, which was held in Los Angeles

71568   HUNTINGTON HOTEL FACING SOUTH, OAK KNOLL, PASADENA, CALIFORNIA

THE GAS BAG IS 150 FEET LONG, 50 FEET IN DIAMETER,
BALLOON CARRIES 10 PASSENGERS AND HAS A LIFTING CAPACITY OF 2200 POUNDS

71210   THE FIRST AMERICAN PASSENGER DIRIGIBLE BALLOON

BATH HOUSE
open every day in the year

SUMMER SCHEDULE:
  Week days   .   .   .   8 a. m. to 11 p. m.
  Sundays   .   .   .   .   8 a. m. to 10 p. m.

WINTER SCHEDULE:
  Week days   .   10 a. m. to 10:30 p. m.
  Sundays   .   .   .   .   8 a. m. to 10 p. m.

BATH HOUSE RATES:
  PLUNGE OR TUB BATH
  including use of suit, towels and room:
  Adults 50c
  Children 25c
  Commutation tickets   .   12 for $4.50

REDONDO BEACH is only an hour's pleasant trip from Los Angeles and is served by two lines of the Pacific Electric Railway.

2303 — AVIATION MEET AT LOS ANGELES, CALIFORNIA.

for your vacation
this summer

Huntington Lake and the High Sierra

Low fares daily **Southern Pacific**

On these pages are some of Henry Huntington's contributions to life in California.

Above: A poster advertising Huntington Lake, a man-made lake in the Sierras, for summer vacations.

Left: A Los Angeles Railway electric trolley car was part of the urban transportation system Henry developed.

Activity: Trace a Trolley Route

The electric trolley system developed by Henry Huntington has been gone for fifty years. The trolleys are gone, but not forgotten. Trace the path of a trolley called the West Adams Blvd. & West Temple St. Route on this map of today's Los Angeles. It began on the corner of Alsace Avenue and Adams Boulevard. Follow the red arrow to this corner and begin tracing the route from here.

- Go east on Adams to Normandie Avenue.
- Turn left on Normandie and go to 24th Street.
- Turn right on 24th and go to Hoover Street.
- Turn left on Hoover and go to Washington Boulevard.
- Turn right on Washington and go one block to Burlington Avenue.
- Turn left on Burlington and go to Venice Boulevard.
- Turn right on Venice and continue until you reach Hill Street.
- Turn left on Hill and continue on to Temple Street.
- Turn left on Temple and follow it to Hoover Street.
- Turn right on Hoover and go to Clinton Street.
- Turn left on Clinton and go to Virgil Avenue.
- Turn right on Virgil and go north to Fountain Avenue.
- Turn left on Fountain and follow it to the end of the line (red dot) on Vermont Avenue. (Today there is a Metro stop two blocks north of this corner on Vermont and Sunset.)

72

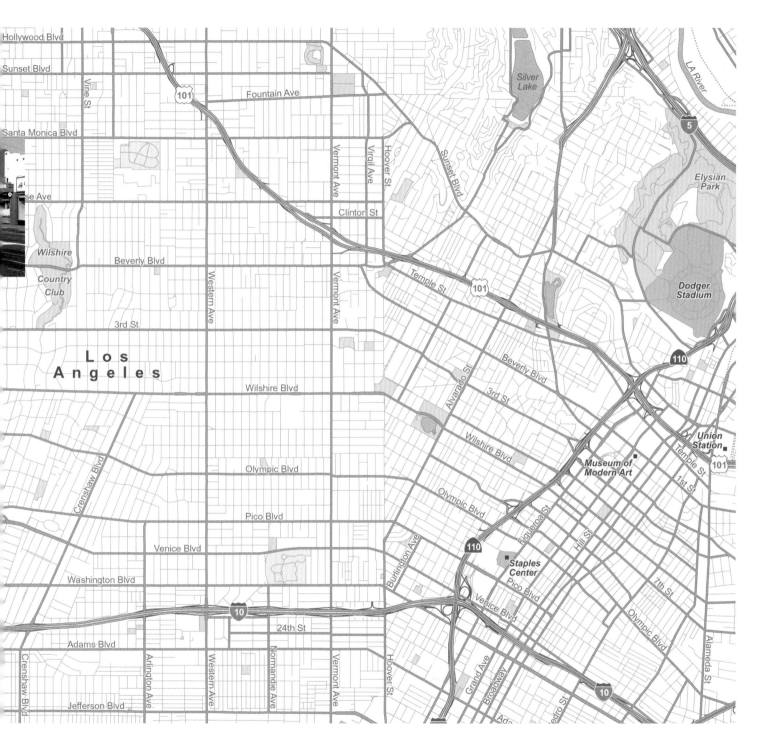

Hollywood Blvd

Sunset Blvd

Vine St

101

Fountain Ave

Santa Monica Blvd

Silver Lake

LA River

5

Vermont Ave

Virgil Ave

Hoover St

Sunset Blvd

Elysian Park

se Ave

Clinton St

Wilshire Country Club

Beverly Blvd

Western Ave

Vermont Ave

Temple St

101

Dodger Stadium

3rd St

Los Angeles

Alvarado St

Beverly Blvd

3rd St

110

Wilshire Blvd

Wilshire Blvd

Union Station

101

Temple St

1st St

Museum of Modern Art

Olympic Blvd

Olympic Blvd

Pico Blvd

Figueroa St

Hill St

Venice Blvd

Crenshaw Blvd

Burlington Ave

110

Staples Center

Pico Blvd

7th St

Washington Blvd

Venice Blvd

Olympic Blvd

10

24th St

Adams Blvd

Arlington Ave

Western Ave

Normandie Ave

Vermont Ave

Hoover St

Grand Ave

Broadway

Pedro St

Alameda St

10

Crenshaw Blvd

Jefferson Blvd

Ada

73